Collect Them All!

Available at bookstores or
directly from Gibbs Smith

1.800.835.4993

www.pocketdoodles.com

animal
doodles
for kids

CHRIS SABATINO

GIBBS SMITH
TO ENRICH AND INSPIRE HUMANKIND

Manufactured in Altona, Manitoba,
Canada in May 2013 by Friesens

First Edition
17 16 15 14 13   5 4 3 2 1

Published by
Gibbs Smith
P.O. Box 667
Layton, Utah 84041

1.800.835.4993 orders
www.gibbs-smith.com

Designed by Melissa Dymock and Virginia Snow

Gibbs Smith books are printed on either recycled, 100%
post-consumer waste, FSC-certified papers or on paper
produced from sustainable PEFC-certified forest/
controlled wood source. Learn more at www.pefc.org.

ISBN 13: 978-1-4236-3457-7

Draw yourself riding this elephant.

Draw the tiger's teeth.

Doodle two big horns on
the rhino's snout.

Draw the animal tracks these explorers are following.

What wild beast is chasing the explorers?

Mongooses hate snakes! Draw the
snake this mongoose is about to fight.

Mongooses travel in groups. Draw who this mongoose is traveling with.

The lion lost the election, so who's the new king of the jungle?

Draw the winner of the Miss Jungle Beauty contest.

What is the photographer shooting?

What is the baboon doodling?

Doodle a cool design on
this leopard's fur.

Give this zebra some new
crazy markings.

Draw the animal who's racing the cheetah.

Doodle the warthog's dinner.

Instead of their normal large, floppy ears, doodle something new on the elephants.

PUPPY EARS

MOOSE ANTLERS

RABBIT EARS

MONKEY
EARS

CAT
EARS

RAM
HORNS

How many monkeys can you doodle on top of this car?

Create a piñata for this animal party.

Who's cleaning the hippo's teeth?

This vampire bat is happy to see the long neck of a giraffe! Draw the giraffe.

Guide the adventurer correctly through the hidden jungle temple maze to find the golden lion statue.

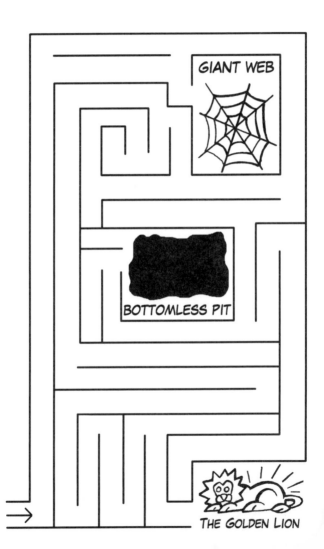

GIANT WEB

BOTTOMLESS PIT

THE GOLDEN LION

While on safari, someone you know
has been grabbed by a giant gorilla!

Draw different pets looking out the windows of this home.

They say people look like their pets.
Draw these pet owners' faces!

Fill the aquarium with goldfish.

This pet rabbit has the
weirdest bunny ears ever!

Finish drawing these house pets.

Guide dogs are trained to lead
blind and seeing-impaired people
around. Draw a friendly guide dog.

Draw the spots on this
firehouse Dalmatian, and give
it a firefighter's hat too!

Draw the animals in the window of the Doodle City Pet Shop!

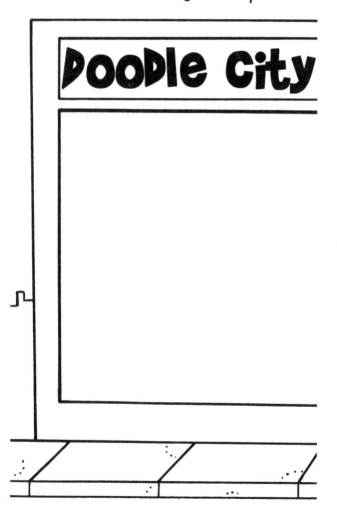

Doodle City

Create a cool house for this gerbil.

Doodle a hamster running on this wheel.

If these pets could talk, what would they say?

Draw the giant hair ball in this cat's stomach.

What is the evil puppy peeing on?

Ferrets love to play. Create a toy
for this ferret to play with.

Draw the scariest house pet ever!

EEK! WHAT IS iT?

Draw this lovebird's mate.

Doodle a pirate on the
parrot's shoulder.

It's raining cats and dogs! Here are the cats; draw the dogs.

Finish this framed picture
of your favorite pet.

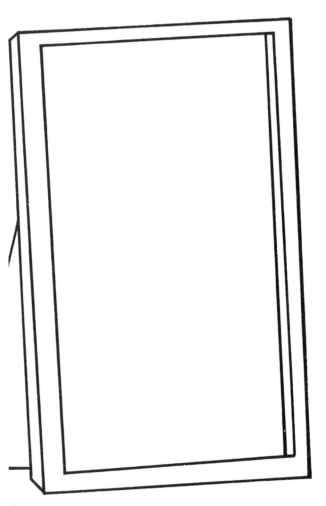

Name this zoo and design the sign at the entrance.

Draw the cutest animal at the zoo.

Draw the scariest animal at the zoo.

Doodle the animal tattoo on this guy's arm.

Create an animal print on this zoo visitor's outfit.

What's the hyena laughing at?

The orangutan is sad today.
Doodle its face.

What's escaping from the zoo?

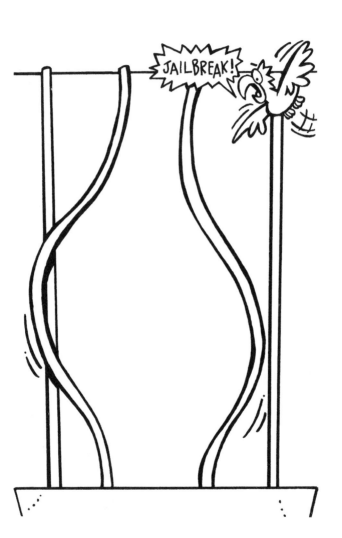

Draw the toucan's big beak!

There's a porcupine in the petting zoo! Doodle pointy quills all over it.

What animal is the zookeeper riding
on the zoo's merry-go-round?

Some chameleons can change color.
Super Chameleon can do more than
that. Draw some cool designs on its skin.

Doodle a design on the peacock's tail feathers.

Draw how the ostrich looks
in the fun-house mirror.

Draw the lion's mane *after* his haircut.

BEFORE

AFTER

What are the zookeeper and the giraffe arguing about?

What is the aardvark in the zoo thinking?

Design your own zoo! Show where each animal should go, and add a gift shop, snack bar, and restrooms.

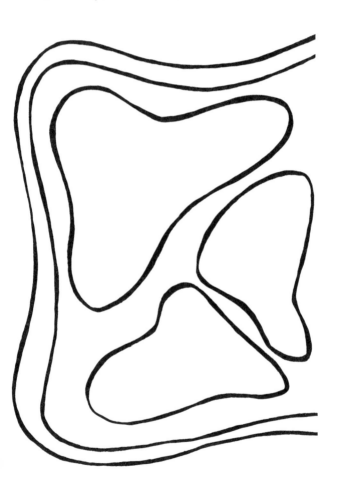

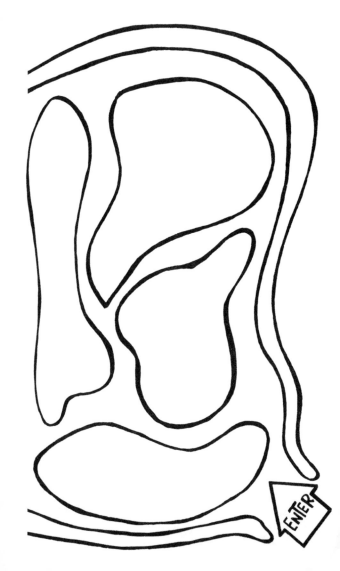

Doodle all the butterflies in the zoo's butterfly house.

THE ZOO IS A WONDERFUL PLACE!

Draw the many different birds
in the zoo's bird exhibit.

THE ZOO IS A WONDERFUL PLACE!

Draw you and your friends taking a
tour of the zoo in the zoo train.

Play a game with a friend on
the tic-tac-toe turtle.

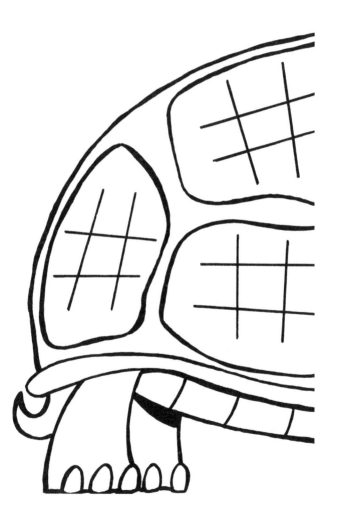

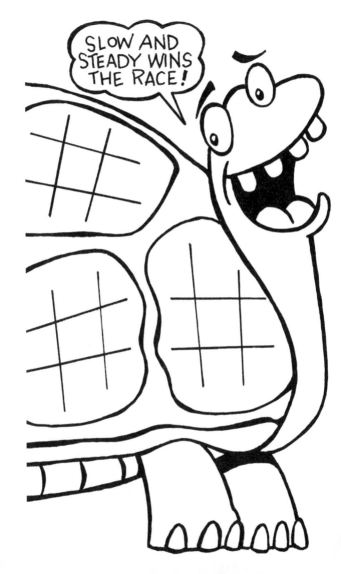

If animals ran the zoo, who would be in the cage?

Doodle an animal from a storybook.

Draw three bears waking up Goldilocks.

Draw the big bad wolf sneaking up on Little Red Riding Hood.

Draw a cow jumping over the moon.

Hey, doodle, diddle! Draw
a cat with a fiddle.

Can you help Bo find her way to her lost sheep?

Draw Humpty Dumpty falling
on these three blind mice.

Draw a sturdy house for these three little pigs that a mean old wolf would have a hard time blowing down.

The princess looks dismayed at what happened after she kissed her boyfriend. Draw him.

Beauty's boyfriend is a real beast! Draw him.

The tortoise and the hare are in
a race. Draw their race cars.

Doodle a great pair of boots on this pussycat.

These three little kittens have
lost their mittens, so draw some
warm clothes on them.

Draw three gruff billy goats
crossing this bridge.

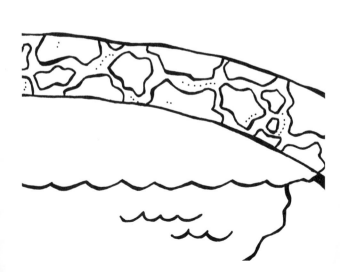

Write your own story about this magical flying puppy.

_____

_____

_____

_____

_____

_____

_____

_____

Doodle a witch's cat.

Draw a wizard's owl.

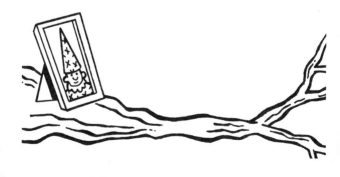

Draw Hickory the mouse running up the side of the clock.

Doodle a pack of rats
following this piper.

Draw the goose that laid
this golden egg.

Draw an animal you've seen
in your own backyard.

Doodle pigeons perched all
over this backyard statue.

What kind of animal is taking a bath in the birdbath?

Draw the garden snake that's fallen in love with this garden hose.

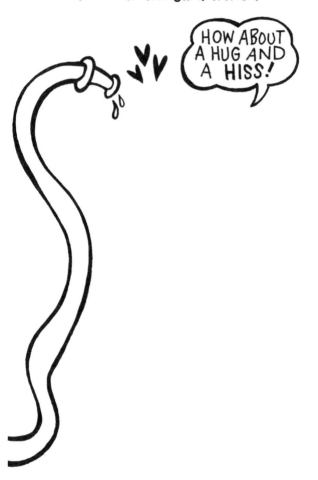

A tree snake is menacing this gardener.
Draw the frightened look on her face.

Draw a family of squirrels living in this tree.

Draw a flying squirrel that's
also a superhero.

ITS A
BIRD!

ITS A
PLANE!

NO! IT'S A
SQUIRREL!

HE'S
NUTS!

What did the animal
control officer catch?

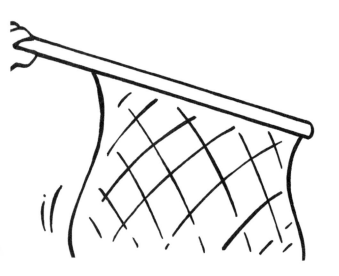

Draw what's in the animal shelter's cages.

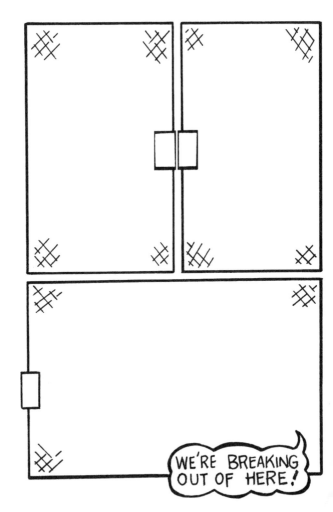

Backyard Bingo. Cross out the
animals you've seen in your yard.

CAT	TURTLE	BIRD
SQUIRREL	FREE SPACE	DUCK
RABBIT	DOG	FOX

Doodle a skunk that doesn't stink.

What is this raccoon stealing
from your trash can?

Draw the flying creature that's ruining this backyard barbeque.

Draw what the woodpecker carved
into the side of this tree.

Draw the different faces of this backyard bunny.

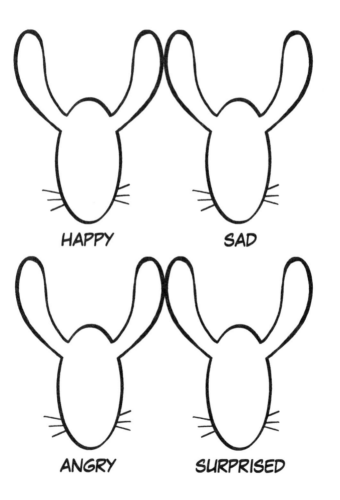

HAPPY

SAD

ANGRY

SURPRISED

Design the inside of the bunny's home down the rabbit hole.

Doodle different animal
tracks in the snow.

Instead of nuts, draw what this smart chipmunk stored for the winter.

What is everyone saying?

Eek! That animal doesn't belong in your backyard.

Doodle work clothes on this farming couple.

Fill the barn with animals.

What do sheep count to fall asleep? Draw them!

Draw who the lamb is fighting with.

Doodle the scarecrow that's protecting this field.

Farmer MacDoodle has trained his animals to help out around the farm. Draw the farm animal that's driving this tractor.

Yes, these pigs are flying—but
they need some wings!

Draw the kind of bank this piggy saves its money in.

The hen planted her eggs in the field. Draw what's growing.

It's the break of dawn. Doodle the rooster that woke you up.

What are the goose and the
turkey eating for lunch?

Draw mama duck's ducklings.

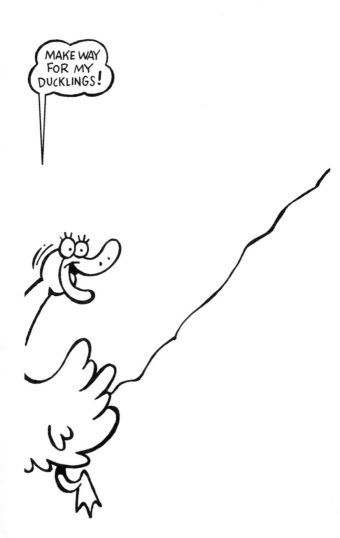

Doodle some animals in the farm pen.

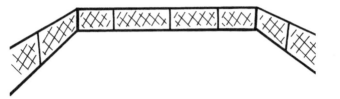

Draw some horses in the field.

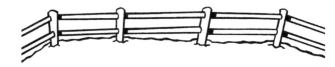

Draw the farm animals' bodies.

COW

PIG

HORSE

GOAT

What's the farmer selling? Draw it.

Draw the animal hitching a ride
in the farmer's wheelbarrow.

Draw the frightened cow these aliens
are beaming up to their flying saucer.

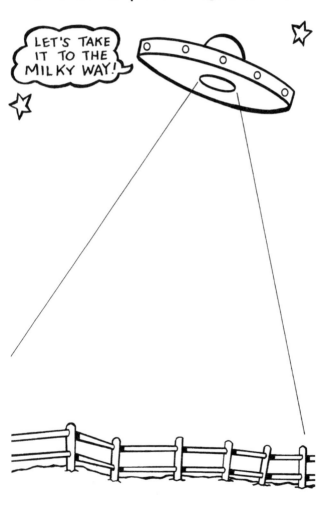

Create a cool design on the side of this cow.

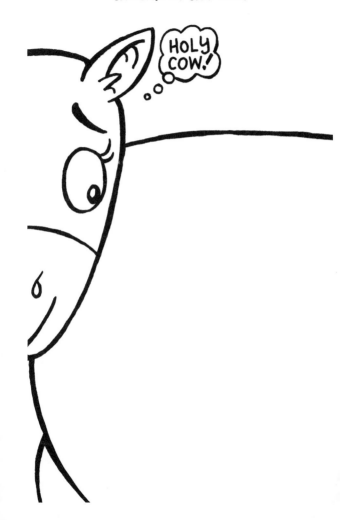

Draw a Frankenstein farm animal made from parts of a horse, goat, sheep, chicken, duck, pig, and cow.

Draw the sea creatures swimming
outside this submarine's porthole.

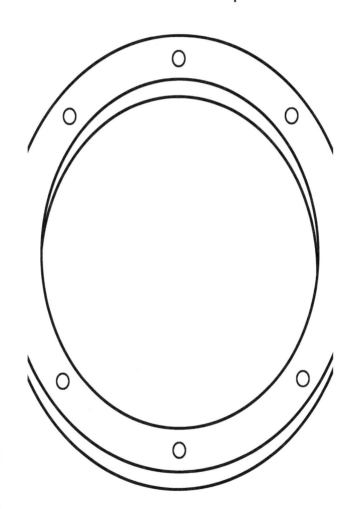

Doodle this shark some big, sharp teeth.

What did the whale swallow?

Turn this starfish into a movie star.

Turn this lobster into a pirate.

Surf's up! Draw the fish riding
the waves on this surfboard.

Doodle eight arms on this octopus.

Draw the sea horse this cowboy crab is riding.

Fill the sky with flying fish.

AT LEAST IT STOPPED
RAINING CATS AND DOGS!

Draw the tails on these cheerleader mermaids.

Create the dogfish the king
of the mermen is walking.

What kind of fish is on the end of this fishing line?

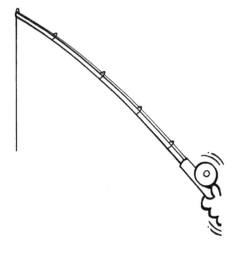

What did the giant squid catch under the sea?

Doodle the rest of this school of fish.

This patriotic beaver built a replica of the Statue of Liberty out of sticks! Draw it.

Draw a large, angry alligator that's not very pleased with this shopper.

An evil witch turned you into a
frog! Draw yourself on a lily pad.

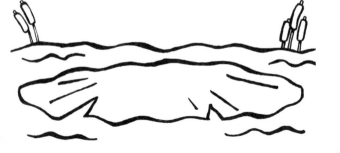

Create a wild sea monster.

Some believe that dolphins talk to each other. What are these dolphins chatting about?

Draw the sheriff of an old Wild West town sitting on his horse.

Draw a coyote howling at the moon.

Draw some prairie dogs
peeking out of their holes.

Horses need horseshoes. Doodle some
appropriate shoes for each horse.

Draw some animals stampeding.

Draw the animal the rodeo clown is riding.

Draw the bull chasing the rodeo clown.

Draw a real cowboy. Create a creature that's half cow and half boy!

Draw a flying buffalo named Bill.
(Don't forget his buffalo wings!)

What did the cowgirl lasso?

Draw all the heavy things
this donkey is carrying!

Finish drawing this poster for the most-wanted billy goat in the West!

WANTED
BILLY the KID

BADDEST GOAT in the WEST!

Fill this desert with rattlesnakes.

Draw the horse that's
pulling the wagon . . .

... and draw all your
friends in the wagon.

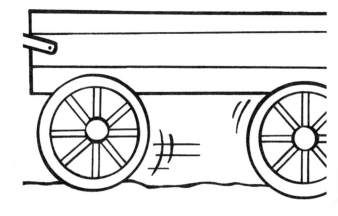

The Pony Express started delivering mail throughout the West in 1860. Create a bridge over the river so the Pony Express rider can get the mail through.

What are the bobcat and the mountain lion using as a scratching post?

What animal is this silly cowboy riding that's making everyone laugh?

What are the polar bears
making out of snow?

Draw who or what the seal
is balancing on its nose.

Draw a sad walrus with crooked teeth in this dentist's chair.

Doodle yourself driving this dog sled . . .

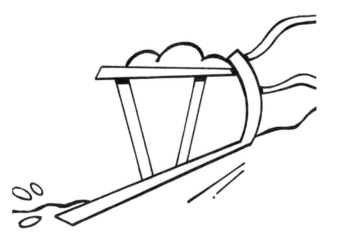

... and draw more dogs
pulling the sled.

Draw Santa's reindeer flying around the Clauses' house.

Draw the animal Jack Frost is riding through the snow.

Draw some penguins playing
hockey on the ice.

A Yeti is said to be a giant, ape-
like snow creature. Draw one.

Draw the forest creature that's
sneaking up on these happy campers.

What is the squirrel doodling
on the back of the bear?

There's a new pest in the forest—part moose and part mosquito! Draw it.

Fill this tree with forest animals.

What animal is scaring
Dorothy in the forest?

What is young wizard Harry Otter conjuring up?

CREATUS MONSTEROSUS!

Doodle oodles of yummy ants all over the anteater's dessert.

Draw the animal the fox reporter is interviewing.

Draw what it is these forest
animals are so happy to see.

A panda bear from China has snuck into the penguin's party. Draw the panda.

Turn this cute koala from
Australia into a scary zombie.

What is this Australian
kangaroo jumping over?

In Canada, reindeer are known as caribous. Draw this caribou's very large antlers.

The wolverine, native to northern areas such as Canada, is very strong despite its small size. Draw what the wolverine is lifting.

Llamas are from South America.
Doodle an outrageous outfit on this
llama so it can enjoy a night out.

Doodle a cool design on this large anaconda from South America.

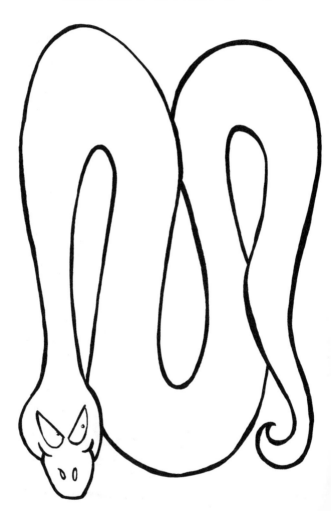

A Komodo dragon is a large lizard
found on islands in Indonesia.
Draw who's chasing it.

This Tasmanian devil is from Australia. Change it into an angel.

Camels are from desert areas.
What are the camel and palm
tree saying to each other?

Create a weird and wild animal completely from your imagination!

Dinosaurs first appeared more than 200 million years ago. Draw a dinosaur body on this history teacher.

Doodle your teacher's head
on this dinosaur body.

Draw as many animals as
you can on Noah's ark.

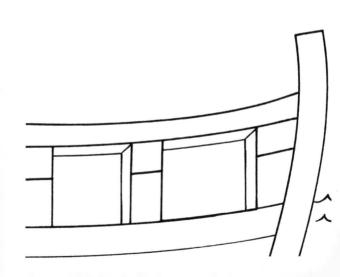

A centaur was thought to be a creature that was half human and half horse. Draw this centaur's horse half.

The legendary unicorn looks like a white horse with a large, pointed horn on its forehead. Draw a magical unicorn.

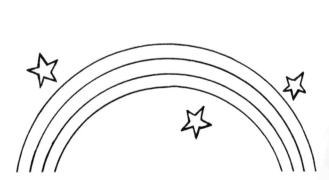

A minotaur was a mythological creature with the head of a bull and the body of a man.

Can you get the minotaur through the labyrinth maze to the exit?

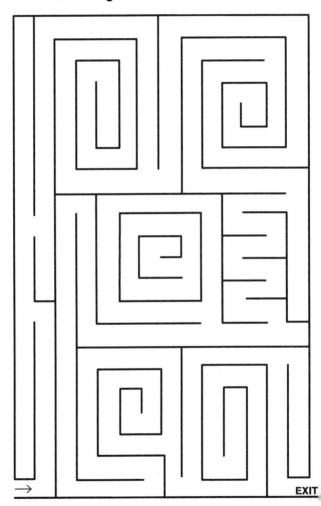

→

EXIT

Medusa was a mythical creature with snakes in place of her hair. Draw the snakes.

Draw a fire-breathing dragon.

DUDE! STOP EATING HOT FOODS AND USE MOUTHWASH!

It's a full moon! Change this
man into a werewolf.

Draw another gargoyle statue sitting on top of this building.

What is the stork carrying in the basket?

It's February 2, Groundhog Day, but the groundhog doesn't see its shadow. What *does* it see?

Animals from outer space have crash-landed on earth. Draw them.

On other planets, we humans are the animals! Draw the aliens watching us.

HUMAN

Add Bigfoot to this family photo.

The legendary Loch Ness Monster of Scotland is reputed to be a giant sea serpent. Draw it sneaking up on this disbelieving scientist.

A griffin is a mythical animal with the head and wings of an eagle and the body and tail of a lion. Finish drawing the griffin.

A harpy is a mythical creature that's part woman and part bird. Add wings, talons, and a tail to the woman below.

Instead of frog legs, doodle the frog a pair of robot legs.

Draw a squid's tentacles on this rabbit.

Doodle this boy some friendly animals
to hang out with so he'll be less lonely.